Secure

How to Have a Healthy Attachment to God

KENZA HADDOCK

Secure: How to Have a Healthy Attachment to God

Published by Aspire Press
An imprint of Tyndale House Ministries
Carol Stream, Illinois
rose-publishing.com

ISBN: 979-8-4005-0015-2

The views and opinions expressed in this book are those of the author(s) and do not necessarily express the views of Tyndale House Ministries or Aspire Press, nor is this book intended to be a substitute for mental health treatment or professional counseling. The information in this resource is intended as a guideline for healthy living. Please consult qualified medical, legal, pastoral, and psychological professionals regarding individual concerns. Tyndale House Ministries and Aspire Press are in no way liable for any content, change of content, or activity for the works listed. Citation of a work does not mean endorsement of all its contents or of other works by the same author.

Printed in United States of America
January 2025, 1st Printing

Contents

I dedicate this book to my heavenly Father, whose faithful love carries me.

Introduction

What Is Attachment?

Real security can only be found in that which can never be taken from you—your relationship with God.

RICK WARREN

In my work as a trauma and pastoral counselor, I discovered that when I helped my clients replace a distorted view of God with the truth about who he is, their anxiety, depression, grief, and other mental health disorders diminished. Such an outcome is not surprising, since God created us for connection with him above all else. Jesus reiterated this when he stated in Matthew 22:37–38, "'Love the Lord your God with all your heart and with all your soul and with all your mind.' This is the first and greatest commandment."

But Jesus also followed that statement with another one about how we are to relate to others: "And the second [greatest commandment] is like [the first]: 'Love your neighbor as yourself'" (Matthew 22:39). You see, it is only *after* we have established a healthy relationship with God that we can cultivate healthy relationships with others. The problem is, we often tend to reverse this order. We prioritize developing healthy relationships with others over establishing a relationship with God as our foundation. When our attempts fail, which they often do, our emotional state can range from frustration and anxiety to depression, grief, and other mental health disorders.

> It is only *after* we have established a healthy relationship with God that we can cultivate healthy relationships with others.

So why do we skip out on having a healthy relationship with God, or even having a relationship with him in the first place? The answer lies in a word that carries much influence throughout our childhood and adult lives: *attachment*. In the mental health world, the concept of attachment refers to the bonding relationship between two people. The development of attachment starts from infancy, when a baby forms a bond with his or her primary caregiver, whether that person is a parent, grandparent, stepparent, or foster parent.

The term *attachment theory* emerged in the 1950s and suggested that the nature of early bonds with caregivers can affect future relationships. Through decades of research, mental health professionals have confirmed that the bonds you formed in your childhood influence how you view yourself and how you currently approach relationships with others and with God. So often if we were raised in an environment where our primary caregiver was either emotionally distant or demanding—or both—we're likely to see God as a bigger version of that person.

Suppose that when you were a child and experienced some kind of physical or emotional pain, your caregiver was in the habit of telling you to stop crying instead of helping you feel better. You went through a repetitive cycle of seeking to be soothed and then being shut down. Now as an adult, when you encounter the pain and confusion that is so much a part of this broken world, you may find yourself repressing your emotions rather than taking healthy steps to seek comfort or help.

It's also interesting to note that the attachment formed with your caregiver is rooted in the reminders and experiences stored in your body's memory, whether healthy or unhealthy. In other words, even before you could speak, your brain was working hard to distinguish between environments that threatened your safety and those that made you feel safe. If your primary caregiver was not in tune with your emotions and did not offer a safe environment in which to express your feelings without judgment or disregard, you likely viewed your authority figures through a negative lens.

> "My people are being destroyed because they don't know me."
> (Hosea 4:6 NLT)

Fast forward to when you were introduced to a relationship with God. If you still had not healed from those childhood experiences, you likely viewed God through the same negative lens, and forming a healthy attachment to him has been a struggle. And while it is true that people with positive caregiver experiences may also have difficulty forming a healthy attachment to God, those cases are far less common.

This brings us back to attachment theory, which identifies several *attachment styles*—short descriptions of the different ways that people approach bonding with others. In *Secure*, you will learn the characteristics of these styles and develop an understanding of how they influence how a person forms an attachment to God. Stories of individuals who experienced each of the unhealthy attachment styles are included to illustrate how misperceptions of God can develop. Also included are "Your Turn" exercises that will help you do the following:

- Identify your own attachment style.
- Realize how your style has affected your behavior, your view of yourself, and your view of God.
- View yourself and God through the lens of truth.
- Move toward developing and maintaining a secure attachment to God.

As we've seen, a misperception of God can undermine not only your relationship with him but also with others, which can ultimately be detrimental to your mental health. As Hosea 4:6 says, "My people are being destroyed because they don't know me" (NLT).

My hope is that no matter what your early attachments were like, you will come to know the truth about God's character and how he sees you. As you do, you will enjoy a close relationship with the one who created the concept of relationships. With a secure attachment to God as your foundation, you will also enjoy the opportunity to experience fulfilling relationships with others.

As you begin your journey, keep in mind the comforting words of Psalm 63:8 (NLT):

> I cling to you [God];
> your strong right hand holds me securely.

Let's get started!

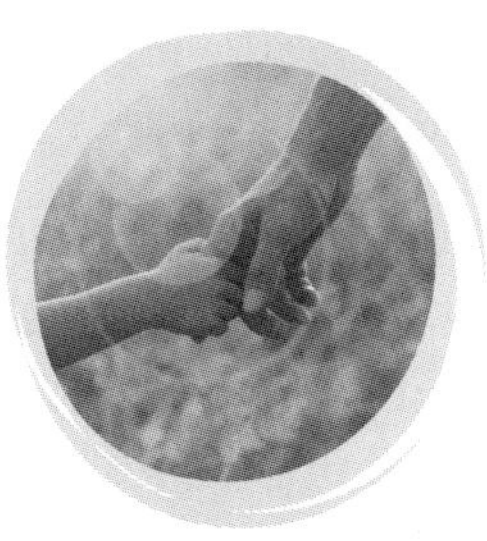

Chapter 1
Unhealthy Attachment Styles and Behaviors

Thank God my salvation does not depend upon my frail hold on Him, but of His mighty grasp on me.

MARTYN LLOYD-JONES

AS WE GROW IN OUR UNDERSTANDING OF THE TERM *attachment*, it's important to recognize that the strength of an attachment depends on the quality of the relationship between the two people sharing a bond. This chapter takes a look at why we can sometimes have a weak attachment to God, based on our early attachment experiences with caregivers.

You'll learn about three types of *unhealthy attachment styles* that people often experience in their formative years, as well as how these styles may affect your attachment with God in the present. You'll also learn about five common behaviors that may result, because we often resort to unhealthy behaviors in an attempt to survive being stuck in a dysfunctional environment with those we are dependent on.

For each attachment style, you'll explore the following:

- What it means
- How it may have affected you
- A case study illustrating its dynamics
- How it can lead to misperceptions about what God is like

As you read, you'll notice the term *unhealthy parent characteristic*, which refers to unhealthy ways that primary caregivers sometimes relate to children. Feel free to substitute the appropriate word that applies to your upbringing—*stepparent*, *grandparent*, *foster parent*, *aunt*, *uncle*, *guardian,* or someone else.

It is also important to note that having a caregiver who displayed some of these characteristics for only brief periods of time does not necessarily mean you developed an unhealthy attachment. It is only when these characteristics are displayed over a long period of time that attachment is negatively affected.

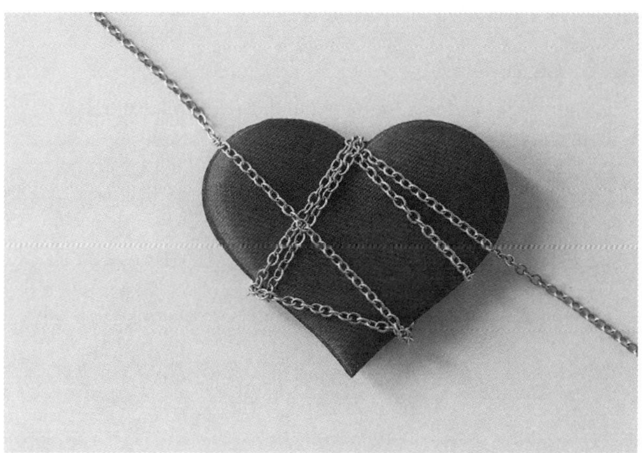

Unhealthy Attachment Styles

1. Avoidant Attachment

According to research, you're more likely to develop an *Avoidant Attachment* style if your parent consistently displayed one or more of the following characteristics.

Unhealthy Parent Characteristic	What It Means	How It Affected You
Emotionally Unavailable	Your parent wasn't available to comfort you when you were in emotional or physical pain.	You felt you weren't worth people's time.
Emotionally Dismissive	Your parent didn't validate your feelings when you felt hurt. In fact, your parent tried to minimize them or claim you were overreacting. You may have gotten in trouble for expressing negative emotions.	You learned to doubt your own feelings. Rather than expressing them, you repressed them, and as a result, you experienced constant inner turmoil.
Overemphasis on Independence	Your parent strongly emphasized that you must become self-reliant, or your parent was annoyed when you needed their help.	You felt that asking for help was wrong and made you look needy.

Case Study: Scott

Scott initially came into therapy for issues related to his marriage and his drinking problem. But as he continued treatment, Scott found out that his main issue ran much deeper: It went back to Scott's dad working two jobs to support the family. When his dad was home, the children were to be quiet and not bother him. "Dad is tired," "Dad had a long day at work," and "Don't bother your dad" were phrases etched in Scott's mind.

Although Scott's mom was present in the home, she was overwhelmed with raising a household of children. Most evenings in Scott's childhood home were chaotic. His mom would be cooking dinner while trying to help his brother with homework; meanwhile, his toddler sister was tugging at his mom for attention. Needless to say, Scott felt it was best to just stay out of her way rather than add one more problem to her plate.

There were instances in seventh grade when Scott told his father he had been bullied in class. Instead of comforting Scott or telling him he would advocate for him at school, Scott's father just shook his head and replied, "If you can't take on a couple of bullies now, how do you plan on making it out in the real world?"

In eighth grade, Scott began to experience anxiety and panic. Having been taught that feeling his emotions meant he wasn't "being a man," he tried his absolute best to repress them. But it seemed the more he did so, the more troubling they became. Scott considered talking to his mom about what he was experiencing, but because she always seemed busy, he decided to keep his thoughts and feelings to himself.

Years later, in an attempt to diffuse conflict in his marriage, Scott started behaving the same way he did when there was conflict in his childhood home. He first tried to avoid it by mimicking the very pattern his father had modeled: working long hours, hoping that if their financial situation improved, his marital issues would disappear. When this didn't pan out, Scott tried hard to ignore his negative emotions because he heard his dad's voice echoing in his mind: *Be a man!* It wasn't long before Scott started drinking alcohol to help numb his feelings.

Scott viewed going to church as an activity to participate in out of tradition. He would take Communion and leave, and he wouldn't think about church again until the following Sunday. Every once in a while, he heard people talk about "walking with God" and "having a relationship with God," but these concepts seemed foreign to him. He didn't understand he could approach God by faith and share his deepest needs and feelings. He didn't know that through Jesus Christ's death on the cross, the door was open to bridge the gap that separated them, allowing him to become a child of God. As a perfect Father, God wanted to comfort Scott with his peace and help him with his problems. Scott knew God was out there, but to Scott, God certainly had better things to do than attend to him.

Misperception of God

He Is Distant

As in Scott's case, having a primary caregiver who is emotionally absent can lead to an Avoidant Attachment style and a perception that God is *distant*. If you have experienced this attachment style, the words "Jesus loves you" or "God is right there with you" may go in one ear and out the other. Your tangible caregiving example can lead you to the erroneous idea that God is busy overseeing the entire universe, so he has no time or interest in adopting a personal concern for you. You believe that God requires you to handle most things on your own, because he doesn't have time for menial problems when he is busy with major issues like wars, poverty, and destructive hurricanes. In your understanding, you should approach God only in times of crisis, and even then, you should not expect him to care about your feelings. The result is that you deny your feelings and live in a state of numbness—and before you know it, numbness has turned into depression.

Unhealthy Parent Characteristic	Misperception of God
Emotionally Unavailable	God is out there somewhere, and I'm over here.
Emotionally Dismissive	God would scoff at my emotions. In fact, if I go to him with my feelings, he may even see me as ungrateful or dramatic.
Overemphasis on Independence	God wants me to have it together before I come to him.

2. Anxious Attachment

At the other extreme is the attachment style known as *Anxious Attachment*. According to research, you are more likely to develop this type of attachment if your parent consistently displayed one or more of the following characteristics.

Unhealthy Parent Characteristic	What It Means	How It Affected You
Clinginess (masked as overprotectiveness)	Your parent was intrusive and lacked boundaries. Even as you got older, your parent had difficulty letting go so that you could learn independence.	You lacked individuality or felt guilty for desiring independence. To appease your parent, you either rebelled to obtain independence or succumbed to your parent's wishes.
Overemphasis on Performance	Your parent put a lot of emphasis on your achievement.	You learned that your worth was tied to how well you succeeded.
High Anxiety	Your parent was anxious, and your parent's own fears were often transmitted to you.	Because your parent's anxiety overwhelmed you, you learned to deal with your parent's emotions by shutting down yours. As a result, you never learned how to process your own emotions in a healthy way.

Case Study: Lilyana

Lilyana was raised in a family that never missed a church service. Their attendance, however, wasn't motivated by their love for God. Rather, Lilyana's grandfather was the pastor of the church, and her dad felt obligated to attend in order to maintain his father's approval. Lilyana learned through her dad's behavior that God required "perfection," including perfect church attendance.

In an effort to drive his point home, Lilyana's dad often quoted the Bible verse that says, "Be perfect ... as your heavenly Father is perfect" (Matthew 5:48). But the truth is that Jesus made this statement in the context of loving those who are considered our enemies. So when Jesus told his disciples to be perfect, he was telling them to imitate their perfect heavenly Father's love. Unfortunately, Lilyana's dad was applying it as a measure of works-based achievement. This led Lilyana to believe she had to work hard, not only to earn God's approval but also to maintain it.

During treatment, Lilyana referenced Bible passages similar to the Matthew 5:48 Scripture, such as Philippians 2:12: "Continue to work out your salvation with fear and trembling." She thought this verse implied that if she did not do enough for God, she could lose his love and, eventually, her status as a child of God. This sent Lilyana into overdrive. She volunteered at church out of fear and made commitments out of guilt. She was stuck in the very cycle from which Jesus died to set her free. Ephesians 2:8–9 makes it clear that we are saved only by God's grace, through faith: "God saved you by his grace when you believed. And you can't take credit for this; it is a gift from God. Salvation is not a reward for the good things we have done, so none of us can boast about it" (NLT).

Misperception of God

He Is Demanding

If you have adopted an Anxious Attachment style and it is not corrected over time, then like Lilyana, you will most likely believe that God is *demanding*. You picture him watching your every move and jotting down your mistakes so he can strike you down for them. Anytime you have a negative thought or feeling, you wonder if God is upset with you. As a result, you live with a sense of ongoing condemnation, like you're forced to keep climbing a steep mountain, never reaching the top. You feel crushed beneath the load of works you must accomplish in order to earn favor with a God who is very difficult to please.

Unhealthy Parent Characteristic	Misperception of God
Clinginess (masked as overprotectiveness)	God is controlling. He's examining me under a microscope.
Overemphasis on Performance	God expects me to be perfect.
High Anxiety	God is angry with me and disappointed in me.

3. Disorganized Attachment

The *Disorganized Attachment* style is the most common one I've seen in the counseling room. It can develop in two ways:

1. One parent was emotionally disconnected, and the other parent tried to make up for it by becoming emotionally enmeshed in your life. You merged both characteristics and attributed them to your current perspective of God.

2. You were raised by a parent whose temperament was like a pressure cooker. Needing to tread carefully to avoid his or her outbursts, you learned to read the room for emotional detonators, so to speak.

Unhealthy Parent Characteristic	What It Means	How It Affected You
Unpredictable Mood Swings	Your parent alternated between intimidation/control and manipulation/guilt-trip tactics.	You felt stuck in fight-or-flight mode because you didn't know what mood your parent would be in on any given day.
Role Reversal (parent relies on child emotionally)	Your parent relied on you for emotional support. Your parent may have used you as a confidant when you were the one in need of someone to lean on.	You developed a habit of assuming responsibility for issues you were not responsible for.
Frequent Criticism and Praise	Your parent was sometimes kind to you and sometimes rejected you or even scared you, depending on whether you were on your parent's "good side" or "bad side."	Your brain was trained to link safety and self-worth with your performance.

WHAT IS FIGHT-OR-FLIGHT MODE?

God created your brain with an emotional wheelhouse called the *amygdala*, which processes your emotions and monitors your safety. When you sense physical or emotional danger, your amygdala activates the *fight-or-flight* response. This causes a hormone called adrenaline to kick in, making you alert and tense, ready to either fight or flee the danger that is confronting you. If you have experienced one of the three unhealthy attachment styles discussed in this chapter, you have likely become accustomed to the need to monitor your surroundings for dangers, whether being alert to tension in a room or people's facial expressions. Living in a fight-or-flight state robs you of the physical, emotional, and mental resources you need to form secure attachments.

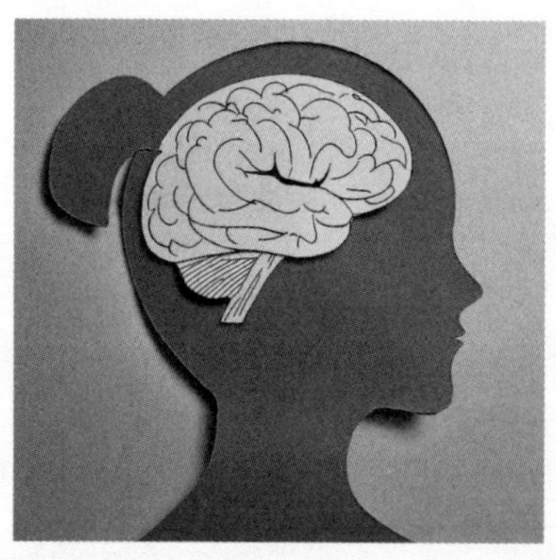

Case Study: Amanda

Amanda's childhood was heartbreaking. She grew up in the foster care system, living in a total of seven homes by the time she aged out of foster care. It started when she lost both of her parents in a tragic car accident. First Amanda lived with her aunt and uncle for a couple of years, where many nights she found herself caught in the middle of their heated arguments. She alternated between refereeing her aunt and uncle and comforting her cousin, who was just a toddler at the time.

When Amanda was nine, her uncle made sexual advances toward her. Amanda told her aunt, who accused her of attempting to break up her marriage. Amanda ended up in foster care, but things were not much better for her there. She was removed from a few homes after it was reported she was being abused. Unfortunately, during the separations, Amanda lost touch with her foster siblings.

One home in particular was especially rough. As Amanda described it, "I didn't know what I was walking into from day to day." She wasn't sure if she would be yelled at for the way she made her bed, or if it was her foster brother's turn to be punished instead. Amanda welcomed sweet relief on the days when she wasn't the one in trouble.

When asked about her relationship with God, Amanda affirmed she believed in God and had attended church on and off throughout her childhood. Amanda's understanding of salvation was summarized in her statement, "You just need to be a good person to get to heaven."

> The Disorganized Attachment style often leads to the belief that God is both *distant and demanding.*

During her time in church, the concept of receiving God's mercy had not been fully explained to her. She knew *about* Jesus, but she did not understand the depth of his love for her, demonstrated by taking the punishment for all of her sins—past, present, and future. Over the course of counseling, Amanda mentioned that she had never actually surrendered her life to his Lordship, because she had served enough "masters" in her lifetime. She wasn't open to the idea of submitting to one more master who might mistreat her the way she had been mistreated in the past.

Misperception of God

He Is Distant and Demanding

When the Disorganized Attachment style is not corrected over time, then like Amanda, you are most likely to believe God is both *distant and demanding*. You fear that at any moment he will get upset with you and punish you. Deep down you want to believe that God cares about you, but it's difficult because throughout your life, you've experienced disappointment and hurt at the hands of an authority figure. It doesn't matter how many times you've heard that God is faithful or has your best interest at heart; there is still a voice in the back of your mind asking, *What if he lets me down? What if he's not who he says he is? What if he ends up being just like so and so, who hurt me? What if ... ?*

Unhealthy Parent Characteristic	Misperception of God
Unpredictable Mood Swings	God is unpredictable and may exhibit his wrath if I approach him at a "bad time."
Role Reversal (parent relies on child emotionally)	God will take away my identity if I commit to him.
Frequent Criticism and Praise	God is not the same all the time, and I never know whether he'll be pleased or angry.

Your Turn

1. Which unhealthy attachment style do you identify with the most, and why?

2. Describe how one of these unhealthy parent characteristics still affects you today.

3. Identify one misperception of God that you have believed. Then spend some time journaling, praying, or talking with a friend about how it has affected your attachment to God.

Unhealthy Attachment Behaviors

The patterns of behavior that accompany unhealthy attachment styles may help us cope in the moment, but as time passes, they actually become a hindrance to our well-being. The next few pages cover five of the most common *unhealthy attachment behaviors* we may acquire while living in an unhealthy attachment setting. You'll learn how these behaviors can affect what we believe about God and how we approach him.

1. Explosion/Implosion

As children, we may not have been able to talk through our negative thoughts and feelings with our caregiver, especially if sharing them would have backfired on us. If we haven't learned how to process them in a healthy way as adults, however, our behavior is affected in one of two ways (or we alternate both):

1. We try to deal with frustration and stress on our own until we can no longer keep it together. Then we emotionally *explode* by yelling or acting out.

2. If we learned from an early age that exploding would threaten our emotional safety, we instead emotionally *implode* by allowing our negative emotions to fester inside of us.

When we explode, we're pushing off emotions we're uncomfortable with by redirecting them toward someone who has nothing to do with the situation. One of my earliest memories of my mom provides an example. When I was about three years old, she was preparing dinner for guests my dad had informed her about at the last minute. Meanwhile, my brother and I were arguing about something. When I came into the kitchen and complained about my brother, my mom flipped the table she was using to peel shrimp. It hurled toward me and knocked my two front teeth loose. Now, as a counselor looking back, I realize my mom was overwhelmed, and I was the unfortunate recipient of her explosion.

When we explode, we're redirecting our emotions toward someone who has nothing to do with the situation.

When we implode, we do the opposite of exploding by keeping our feelings to ourselves. We may look calm on the outside, but inside we're in turmoil. Rather than redirecting our pent-up emotions toward someone else (exploding), we direct them toward ourselves. In other words, we explode on ourselves on the inside. As a result, we often experience what mental health professionals refer to as *psychosomatic symptoms*. This is a fancy way of describing physical ailments caused by not releasing emotional distress: headaches, stomachaches, panic attacks, or other symptoms that have no medical basis.

Both exploding and imploding impede our ability to develop a healthy attachment to God. When we redirect our emotions toward someone else (exploding), we've determined it isn't safe to express to God how we truly feel. When we stuff our emotions (imploding), we're writing God off as someone who doesn't care about us. The problem is that healthy attachment requires a willingness to be transparent about our emotions. But if we've spent years fearing that acknowledging our feelings to God would result in pain or even his rejection, then we would likely settle for a superficial attachment to God—going through the motions of religious duties so we can "get him off our back."

2. Withdrawal

An environment that restricted you from sharing your thoughts and feelings may have also prompted you to *withdraw* from people and activities. In the present day, you may find yourself falling into the habit of trying to solve problems on your own. If you grew up in an environment that was chaotic and overwhelming, today when you experience the same circumstances, you are likely physically present in the situation but mentally checked out.

For example, let's say you signed up to serve in multiple areas at church, but now you're in a life transition that necessitates dropping a few ministry commitments. If you believe that God loves you more when you're serving, or if you equate having a healthy attachment to God with being in ministry, you're likely to keep pushing yourself beyond burnout. Feeling guilty that you've lost your passion for serving, you withdraw mentally; but you're present physically, going through the motions. You feel stuck because you believe the quality of your relationship with God is contingent on your service at church.

3. Numbing

Numbing means that you pick a certain vice—whether a thing or a person—to become your "escape" from reality. Numbing your emotions is a way of resisting having to confront how you feel, especially if you were never taught how to process your thoughts and emotions in a healthy way. Methods for numbing can differ depending on the stage of life you're in. Children who feel overwhelmed by an environment they're unable to escape might watch TV or play video games for hours. For adults, numbing can take the form of drinking too much alcohol or engaging in substance abuse. Other examples include overeating, spending an excessive amount of time in front of a screen, and putting all of one's energy into work.

4. Excessive Compliance

If your caregiver had mood swings that threatened your emotional safety, it's possible you became *excessively compliant* by obeying their instructions and accepting their beliefs, even if you disagreed. You carefully chose your words to prevent emotional outbursts, and you paid more attention to your caregiver's emotions than to your own.

Carrying this behavior into how you relate to God means that he also becomes someone to say yes to, but only because you're afraid of what might happen if you ask questions. Overcompliance happens when you believe you're not allowed to ask God questions. You see God as someone who requires blind trust. Therefore, you may oblige out of fear, but internally you are trembling and waiting for the floor to cave in. In other words, you fear God, but you don't trust him.

5. Quiet Defiance

Quiet defiance is also characterized by compliance, but in this case you do what you want when no one else is looking. I once had a client, Kate, who was raised in a very strict home and fit this criteria from childhood into her adult life. Her parents meant to protect her, but they did so by enforcing rules rather than cultivating a meaningful relationship as a foundation for those rules. Kate was polite and knew exactly what to say and do to fly under her parents' radar. For example, she would often dress conservatively for school but secretly pack the clothes she really wanted to wear in her backpack. When she arrived at school, she would change into the new outfit.

"Why didn't you just leave for school with the outfit you wanted to wear?" I asked.

"Are you kidding?" she replied. "Have you met my dad? He would've read me the riot act!"

This sentence sums up how Kate viewed her dad.

As she grew older, Kate never missed church, but her heart wasn't there. Most of her time sitting in a pew was spent texting a guy she'd met at a club the night before.

"Why did you keep going to church if your heart wasn't really in it?" I once asked during our session.

"Because that's just what I was raised to do," she said.

"Do you spend time with God?" I asked.

"Yes, I go to church on Sundays," she replied.

"No, I mean outside of church," I clarified.

"Huh? How do you mean?" she asked.

As our conversation continued, it became evident that although Kate had gone to church and attended church activities when she was growing up, she had not yet established a bond or attachment with God. That component was missing because Kate had a counterfeit image of God in her mind—just as I once did, and maybe you did as well. Her parental example led her to believe that God was distant and demanding, so she reacted with quiet defiance.

■ ■ ■

FIVE COMMON UNHEALTHY ATTACHMENT BEHAVIORS

1. Explosion/Implosion
2. Withdrawal
3. Numbing
4. Excessive Compliance
5. Quiet Defiance

Regardless of your attachment style and any unhealthy behaviors that may have resulted, it's no accident that you're reading this book. And regardless of any misperceptions you may have about God, the truth is that he loves you, cares about you, and has been pursuing you. Part of his pursuit involves revealing to you who he truly is. There never could be enough pages to describe all of God's great qualities, so for the purpose of this book, the next chapter presents three of his main attributes. Understanding these truths about his character, as well as knowing the truth about yourself and how God sees you, is an important step in developing a healthy attachment to him.

Your Turn

1. Which unhealthy attachment behavior do you resort to most often?

2. Describe a time from your childhood when you exhibited this behavior with someone in authority.

3. How has this behavior affected your attachment to God?

Chapter 2
The Truth about God and Yourself

What comes into our minds when we think about God is the most important thing about us.

A. W. TOZER

UNHEALTHY ATTACHMENT STYLES AND BEHAVIORS may be part of our past, but they don't have to influence our future. When we understand the truth about God's character, we can start to build a healthy, secure attachment to him that will also provide a solid foundation for healthy relationships with others.

In this chapter we'll cover three important attributes of God, as well as three important truths about how he sees you.

As you read, allow your perceptions of God to be transformed, and take delight in understanding your identity as his child. Allow God's very own words, as written in the Bible, to bring your thoughts into alignment with his perfect truth. God created you with billions of nerve cells that are actively working to make new connections in your brain, so the more truth you learn about these important topics, the more your brain will make positive associations with God. This will help guide your heart and emotions toward a secure attachment to him.

Allow your perceptions of God to be transformed, and take delight in understanding your identity as his child.

The Truth about God

1. He Is a Merciful Judge

As part of an unhealthy early-attachment experience, did you ever liken a strict authority figure in your life to a mean, cold judge who was waiting for you to mess up? If so, you now understand how easy it is to see God as a bigger version of this "judge" who is eager to lecture you or punish you. I have seen so many people come in for treatment who grew up with this misperception. Some of them even grew up in church and believed they needed to have perfect lives before God would accept them.

Take Nichole, for example. She initially came to counseling seeking relief from anxiety, but discussing her faith journey actually made her more anxious than peaceful. She recalled how she grew up believing that God expected her to be perfect. She imagined God was like a harsh judge holding a gavel, ready to slam it down because he was upset with her. And like Amanda in the previous chapter, she was too tired to appease one more demanding person in her life.

Now, there is no denying that God is a judge. The Bible says, "Let the heavens proclaim his justice, for God himself will be the judge" (Psalm 50:6 NLT). Since God made heaven and earth and everything in between, including you and me, he is the "owner" who gets to set the standard for what is right and wrong. He alone is the Holy Judge. God's standard of holiness means that if we were to die without his forgiveness for our sins, we would be separated from him forever in a place called hell, where there is "weeping and gnashing of teeth" (Luke 13:28 NLT). God would be completely justified in allowing this, yet in his love he made a way for us to receive mercy.

To illustrate, let's go back to Nichole. As she and her counselor worked on repairing her attachment to God, she just couldn't shake her image of God as a mean, cold judge. Then her counselor shared a story with her that I would like to share with you:

> Imagine you are driving on a highway, listening mindlessly to the radio. At one point you look in the rearview mirror and see those dreaded lights flashing behind you. You quickly glance at your speedometer and realize you're going over the speed limit. You get a ticket, and after a few months pass, your court date arrives. You get to court and wait with dread. When your name is called, you approach the judge, heart pounding. The judge asks, "How do you plead?"
>
> You know you're guilty. As you stand before the judge for what seems like forever, desperate thoughts come to your mind: *Should I lie? Should I say I was late for work? Should I say my speedometer was broken? My friend Michael's friend is a mechanic—maybe he could back me*

> *up!* You start running out of excuses and look up into the judge's piercing eyes. Your voice shakes as you reply, "I plead guilty. I'm so sorry, your honor."
>
> All of a sudden, the judge's expression shifts. His brows relax and his eyes hold a hint of warmth. He writes something on a slip of paper, leans forward slightly, and hands the note to you. You anxiously read his words and are shocked to learn that he has dropped the case! Your record is clear, as if you were never caught speeding. The judge had every right to issue you a hefty penalty, but instead, he showed you mercy.

In the same way, God, who has the right to judge and condemn us, has made a plan of redemption for us—and that plan is believing in Jesus Christ, the Son of God, for the forgiveness of our sins. John 3:16–18 describes God's loving, merciful, gracious nature this way:

> This is how God loved the world: He gave his one and only Son, so that everyone who believes in him will not perish but have eternal life. God sent his Son into the world not to judge the world, but to save the world through him. There is no judgment against anyone who believes in him. But

anyone who does not believe in him has already been judged for not believing in God's one and only Son. (NLT)

Whether or not we trust in Jesus, God remains the judge. But when we admit our sinfulness to Jesus, God becomes a judge *on our side*. God, the rightful judge, now looks at us through eyes of mercy. The Bible says it this way: "There is no condemnation for those who belong to Christ Jesus" (Romans 8:1 NLT). Since God's judgment for sin fell on Jesus when he was crucified, we who surrender our lives to Jesus get to experience God as a judge who is merciful, though his standard for holiness doesn't change. To learn more about this, see the sidebar "What Is a 'Relationship with God'?" at the end of this section.

MERCY AND RIGHTEOUSNESS

Showing *mercy* means withholding punishment that is rightfully deserved.

- "Because of his great love for us, God, who is rich in mercy, made us alive with Christ even when we were dead in transgressions." (Ephesians 2:4-5)

God knows that in our human weakness we struggle with sin, so in his mercy, he sent Jesus to give us the *righteousness* of God.

- "God made him who had no sin to be sin for us, so that in him we might become the righteousness of God." (2 Corinthians 5:21)

2. He Is a Faithful Friend

"Friend" is one of God's most inviting attributes. Romans 5:10 says, "Our friendship with God was restored by the death of his Son while we were still his enemies" (NLT). For those who accept Christ's forgiveness, God becomes not only a judge on their side but also a faithful friend. This does not mean that friendship with him exempts us from the hardships of life, but it does assure us of his presence through it all. Jesus says in Matthew 28:20, "Surely I am with you always, to the very end of the age." It's so comforting to know that we are never alone!

When things aren't going as planned, however, it's still easy to think that Jesus has forsaken us when we need him most. We may feel angry, upset, and hurt—and even guilty for feeling that way. If we don't have a secure attachment to Jesus, we can get stuck in a constant state of turmoil where we bottle up our emotions, then explode and feel bad for exploding, then go back to bottling up our emotions and repeating the cycle. Sound familiar?

In John 15:14, Jesus says, "You are my friends if you do what I command." Friendship with Jesus means that we can be transparent with him. He will not get angry when we come to him and share our real feelings—even when we're disappointed that he hasn't answered our prayers as we hoped he would. We can also come to him for guidance when making decisions. After all, what seems like common sense in the natural world does not always equal common sense in the supernatural. Through the counsel of his Word and his Holy Spirit, Jesus helps us make decisions that are in line with his will for our lives.

Friendship with Jesus means that we can be transparent with him.

Of course, we still need the support and help of our earthly friends, so let the guidance of the Holy Spirit be the foundation upon which you build your other friendships. Ask God to give you friendships that will empower you and spur you toward Christ. Healthy earthly friendships are actually another important way through which God demonstrates his own friendship toward you. When a friend sends an encouraging text, offers a listening ear when you've had a tough day, or babysits your kids so you can recharge or run to an appointment, that friend is a tangible manifestation of God's care for you.

GOD AS FRIEND

- Through his Holy Spirit, God is with us through good times and bad.
- It is safe to tell God about our feelings, even when we are disappointed or angry with him.
- God wants to guide our decisions.
- God also demonstrates his friendship through the caring actions of others.

3. He Is a Loving Father

When God is a judge on your side, he becomes not only a faithful friend but also your loving heavenly Father who cares for your every need. But if your primary caregiver did not always have your best interest at heart, you may see God the Father as someone who doesn't truly care for you as much as he cares about what you do for him. As a result, you regard spending time with God as a chore rather than a privilege. Because you see it as a chore, you start dreading the thought of nurturing your attachment to him through prayer and Bible reading.

If this resonates with you, please don't feel ashamed, because I've been there, and I can attest that many of my clients have been there too. It is such a common feeling and stems from a lack of understanding of the depth of God's love for us. I have found it's much easier to help someone view God as a judge on their side or as a caring best friend than to help them see God as the grace-filled Father that he is. So many of us had fathers with unhealed emotional wounds, lacking the capacity to nurture and protect us the way God intended.

The truth is that God is the most caring and protective Father we could ever have. Think of someone who has always been encouraging to you, someone you felt you could be yourself with—who has seen you at your worst but is not going anywhere. Now multiply that kind of love by infinity, and that's the extent of the Father's love toward *you*! Take a look at the following list of ways that God demonstrates the depth of his fatherly love toward us.

- *He pursues us*—"The Son of Man came to seek and to save the lost." (Luke 19:10)
- *He calls us to himself*—"He has saved us and called us to a holy life—not because of anything we have done but because of his own purpose and grace." (2 Timothy 1:9)
- *He redeems us*—"When the set time had fully come, God sent his Son, born of a woman, born under the law, to redeem those under the law, that we might receive adoption to sonship." (Galatians 4:4–5)
- *He welcomes us in our mess*—"God demonstrates his own love for us in this: While we were still sinners, Christ died for us." (Romans 5:8)
- *He gives us worth that no one can ever take from us*—"'Though the mountains be shaken and the hills be removed, yet my unfailing love for you will not be shaken nor my covenant of peace be removed,' says the LORD, who has compassion on you." (Isaiah 54:10)

God is committed to walking with you through the process of learning who he really is as your Father. This may not be easy, depending on what your childhood history looks like, but he isn't surprised by the baggage you come to him with. In fact, part of developing a relationship with God as your heavenly Father is learning to trust him with the parts you don't like about yourself.

This is the process that God the Father walked Jon through years ago. He was raised by a father who struggled with alcoholism and a hot temper, which kept Jon on edge every day. As you can imagine, Jon's brain remained in constant fight-or-flight mode. Because of this experience, Jon resented all authority figures, including God. As an adult, Jon, too, became stuck in the destructive cycle of alcoholism—the very thing he'd promised to avoid. It was so bad that the court ordered him to receive therapy.

God is committed to walking with you through the process of learning who he really is as your Father.

During our first few sessions, Jon was closed off, angry that the very person who was supposed to protect him and model God's love had failed him miserably.

I told Jon he needed to process the chaotic past that had left his heart shattered in pieces. Jon proceeded very cautiously with me as I walked him through an exercise that helped him see the contrast between his dad and God the Father. (If you would like to walk through this same exercise, take a look at Exercise 1 in the appendix: "Know God as a Loving Father.")

Jon eventually surrendered his life to Jesus, acknowledging him as Lord and accepting his gift of salvation. Even after he began his walk of faith with God, Jon still experienced moments where he doubted God's love for him. But as the years went on, Jon's confidence in God became greater, and his depression and anger gradually lessened as his relationship with God deepened. He came to know God as the loving Father that he truly is.

WHAT IS A "RELATIONSHIP WITH GOD"?

What does it mean to "have a relationship with God" or to "know God"? First, we must have God as a ***judge*** on our side, since he alone is perfect and has the right to judge our actions, thoughts, and attitudes. This happens when we surrender our lives to Jesus, admitting that only Jesus's death and resurrection earn our forgiveness, giving us the right to be called children of our heavenly Father.

When we receive God's forgiveness and spend time with him through prayer and Bible reading, we gradually leave behind our misperceptions and come to know God as a trusted ***friend*** and loving ***Father***. Through his Holy Spirit, he assures us of his presence and gives us comfort and guidance. If you do not yet know God in this way but would like to, consider this prayer as a first step:

> Lord Jesus, I confess that I am a sinner in need of a Savior. Thank you for dying on the cross to forgive me and become a judge on my side. I surrender my life to you as my Lord and Savior. Please draw me close to you and help me to see you as the faithful friend and loving Father that you truly are. Amen.

Your Turn

1. How does viewing God as a judge on your side change your perspective of him?

2. List some ways you have experienced God as a friend. For each instance, thank him for his care.

3. Which aspect of God's fatherly love that we discussed (pursuing you, calling you to himself, redeeming you, etc.) resonates with you the most, and why?

The Truth about Yourself

Knowing the truth about God's attributes is vital for having a secure attachment to him, but equally important is knowing the truth about yourself.

Everywhere you look, people are trying to answer the question, "Who am I?" Looking to others for answers has proven unsuccessful, because often people don't even know themselves. Mental health professionals sometimes recommend searching within ourselves for answers, but since we did not create ourselves, this is not a logical method.

Because God made us, only he can tell us the truth about who we are. The Bible reveals how God defines us, so let's take a look at some important Scripture passages that will help us see how, when we become God's children, we are *chosen*, *forgiven*, and *treasured* by him. We are no longer defined by negative experiences with our parents or mistreatment by a friend. Rather, we are defined by the One who calls us by name. In Romans 8:29–30 we read,

> God knew his people in advance, and he chose them to become like his Son, so that his Son would be the firstborn among many brothers and sisters. And having chosen them, he called them to come

to him. And having called them, he gave them right standing with himself. And having given them right standing, he gave them his glory. (NLT)

Over the next few pages, we're going to break down what this passage means about our identity in Christ. I pray that as you read, God will open your heart to understand the way he sees you through the sacrifice that Jesus accomplished on your behalf.

1. You Are Chosen

"God knew his people in advance, and he chose them to become like his Son." **(Romans 8:29 NLT)**

One of our greatest human needs is to be assured that we bring meaning to another person's life. If you've struggled with attachment issues, you most likely grew up in an environment where you felt you were unimportant or an inconvenience—one where your presence didn't make a difference. This only strengthened your need to be seen and chosen by someone.

King David, one of the Bible's heroes, had a similar experience. His father, Jesse, overlooked David when the prophet Samuel came to choose the next king of Israel from among Jesse's eight sons. Jesse did not even invite David to be considered, perhaps because David was the youngest or was "just" a shepherd boy.

When Samuel observed the fine features of one particular son of Jesse, he thought that surely God would choose him as king. But God said to Samuel, "Don't judge by his appearance or height, for I have rejected him. The LORD doesn't see things the way you see them. People judge by outward appearance, but the LORD looks at the heart" (1 Samuel 16:7 NLT).

> One of our greatest human needs is to be assured that we bring meaning to another person's life.

One by one, each of Jesse's sons, except David, was presented to Samuel. But Samuel told Jesse that the Lord had not chosen any of them. Jesse had thought at least one of these sons was fit to be king, but God had other plans. When Samuel asked if Jesse had any other sons, Jesse remarked that David was out in the fields, looking after the sheep and goats. After Jesse sent for David, the Lord told Samuel, "This is the one" (1 Samuel 16:12 NLT).

Just as he chose David to be king, God chose you to be his child—not out of obligation but simply because he wanted to. Ephesians 1:5 says that "God decided in advance to adopt us into his own family by bringing us to himself through Jesus Christ. This is what he wanted to do, and it gave him great pleasure" (NLT).

This truth might make you uncomfortable because it seems counterintuitive—especially if you had to vie for your caregiver's attention, prove your worth, or work hard to be noticed. But the story about God's choice of David is a reminder that God started pursuing you before you even knew to seek him. My friend, you may never experience someone choosing you for that promotion or special opportunity you wanted, but you can rest assured that the King of kings has chosen you for an honored status you could never have attained by yourself: *child of God*.

2. You Are Forgiven

"Having called them, [God] gave them right standing with himself." **(Romans 8:30 NLT)**

When you became a child of God, your sins were forgiven and wiped clean. This is such an amazing truth to grasp that it almost seems too good to be true. Remembering your past mistakes is one obstacle that can make it difficult to believe you stand justified before God. Another is when friends or family continue to bring up your past because they don't understand how Christ's sacrifice has dealt with it once and for all.

This was Ashley's ongoing turmoil. She lost her father at a young age, and as a teenager, she made decisions that got her into trouble. Suicide attempts eventually led her to spend time in inpatient mental health facilities. During one stay, Ashley met a friend who told her about Jesus. She started attending a Bible study and soon surrendered her life to Jesus.

When you became a child of God, your sins were forgiven and wiped clean.

Ashley worked hard to rebuild her life, but her mom continued to hold Ashley's past over her head, frequently bringing it up at family events or gossiping about her to others. Ashley felt defeated. She wondered if her mom would ever see her as "good enough" or stop comparing her to her siblings, who didn't have a colorful past like she did. Ashley often said, "It doesn't matter how much I try; my mom seems to always pull me right back down."

As I listened to Ashley, it was evident that although she had a relationship with God, she was still carrying shame from her past. I walked her through an exercise where she wrote down the worst sins she had ever committed and acknowledged the shame she felt. She made up her mind to receive God's forgiveness for each one, then expressed her gratitude to God.

When we bring shame to the surface and allow ourselves to receive God's forgiveness, shame's power over us is weakened. If you wonder whether you will ever stop being haunted by past mistakes, I'd like to encourage you to complete Exercise 2 ("Believe You Are Forgiven") in the appendix. Also, thoughtfully consider how the following Scriptures testify to the truth that if you are a believer and follower of Jesus Christ, you are justified and forgiven before God:

- "Since we have been justified through faith, we have peace with God through our Lord Jesus Christ." (Romans 5:1)

- "Since we have now been justified by [Christ's] blood, how much more shall we be saved from God's wrath through him!" (Romans 5:9)
- "[God] saved us through the washing of rebirth and renewal by the Holy Spirit, whom he poured out on us generously through Jesus Christ our Savior, so that, having been justified by his grace, we might become heirs having the hope of eternal life." (Titus 3:5–7)

3. You Are Treasured

"Having given them right standing, he gave them his glory." **(Romans 8:30 NLT)**

In addition to choosing you and wiping your slate clean, God honors and treasures his relationship with you. He even shares his glory with you!

Another way of saying you are treasured is to say that you are cherished. When someone cherishes you, they want to spend time with you. They want to show you how much they love you and to remind you how special you are. Have you ever noticed how two people who are in love look at each other? The moment they lock eyes, it's like they are the only two people in a crowded room. My friend, that's how God looks at you.

We tend to focus on attributes of God like his sovereignty and might, yet we forget to highlight how relational he is. Yes, God is sovereign over the entire universe, and at the same time, he loves you enough to pay special attention to you. Zephaniah 3:17 says, "He will rejoice over you with joyful songs" (NLT). Think of a mother rocking her baby boy to sleep—singing to him, delighting in him, and caressing his head. That's how gentle God is with you.

> Another way of saying you are treasured is to say that you are cherished.

God tenderly cares for you. He knows you have tried to hide your vulnerabilities because of how helpless you have felt at times in your life. Because he treasures you, he wants you to take one step closer to him today. You may not be able to let your guard down fully, but for now, know that he wants you to come to him with your pain, shame, and doubt. Come to him regardless of how messed up you may feel, trusting in these words of Jesus: "Those the Father has given me will come to me, and I will never reject them" (John 6:37 NLT).

TREASURED BY GOD

- "The LORD has declared today that you are his people, his own special treasure, just as he promised." (Deuteronomy 26:18 NLT)
- "Can a woman forget her nursing child? Can she feel no love for the child she has borne? But even if that were possible, I would not forget you!" (Isaiah 49:15 NLT)
- "You are God's chosen treasure–priests who are kings, a spiritual 'nation' set apart as God's devoted ones." (1 Peter 2:9 TPT)

Your Turn

1. How does the fact that God has chosen you help you to approach him with more boldness?

2. Which Scripture about God's justification and forgiveness resonates with you the most, and why?

3. Write out one or more of the Scriptures listed in the sidebar "Treasured by God." Then ask God to show you specific ways in which he treasures you personally.

Chapter 3
Moving to Secure Attachment

A God wise enough to create me
and the world I live in is wise
enough to watch out for me.

PHILIP YANCEY

ONCE WE UNDERSTAND THAT AS A JUDGE ON OUR side, God truly is a faithful friend and loving Father who chooses, justifies, and treasures his children, the question becomes, *How can we progress from acting out patterns of fear and uncertainty to cultivating a secure attachment with God and others?*

In Colossians 3:20, the apostle Paul summarizes the heart of what secure attachment looks like between a child and a parent, which was intended to reflect the secure attachment we would ultimately have with God as our heavenly Father. It reads, "Children, obey your parents in everything, for this pleases the Lord."

How can we apply this principle to our relationship with God? How do we obey him "in everything"? For starters, Hebrews 11:6 says that "without faith it is impossible to please God." We can choose to draw near to God through faith in his loving nature.

This chapter discusses three layers of attachment that, as we choose to move through them by faith, will ultimately move us to a place of full trust and security in God. Next, we need to maintain that attachment through obedience to the principles in his Word. Jesus said in John 14:15, "If you love me, keep my commands." When we prioritize God in our lives in this way, we are living a life of secure attachment, filled with love for God and others.

We can choose to draw near to God through faith in his loving nature.

Layers of Attachment

In order to love God, we must first learn to open our hearts to him. It doesn't happen all at once but rather one step and one layer at a time. Imagine a heart who is excited to see you, with three layers: (1) outer, (2) middle, and (3) core:

We begin with the outer layer, where we learn to feel emotionally safe with God. As we feel comfortable, we move to the middle layer, where we become transparent with God about our true selves. Finally, we move to the inner core, where we establish a secure attachment with God by fully entrusting ourselves to his care.

1. Emotional Safety

The process of building a secure attachment with God starts with learning to have simple conversations with him through prayer. At first you are likely to "tiptoe" around God as you approach him in these conversations, trying to figure out if he is truly loving. Remember how in chapter 1 we discussed the amygdala—the emotional wheelhouse of your brain? When you start tapping into this first phase of secure attachment to God, your amygdala is scanning for emotional safety. After you begin talking with him through prayer, you will discover that you don't need to fear a hurtful response.

Be Yourself

In these conversations, you don't have to use proper words or phrase things a certain way. Simply talk with God just like you would talk to a friend. Even more than that, he is your heavenly Father. It may feel awkward at first, but don't give up trying. Consider a few of the following prayer-conversation starters:

- List a few people or things you're thankful for today, and why you're grateful for each one: "Father, I'm thankful for _______________ because _____________________________."
- Share about your day as you would with a friend: "God, today I ___________________ ________________________."
- Tell him what is overwhelming you or making you anxious: "Father, I'm so anxious about ___________________________."
- Tell him about a situation where someone upset you: "Father, I'm so angry with __________ for ____________________."

After you talk to God, I encourage you to wait a few moments as you practice listening for how he will respond. God may bring a memory to your mind. He may give you peace about your circumstances. He may give you knowledge about a situation. You may feel either a sense of freedom or a sense of caution about proceeding with certain plans.

Whatever it is, keep this in mind: As his child, God will never make you feel anxious or condemned. And if you don't get a sense that God is responding to you right away, don't worry. I've experienced times when the Lord responded through a passage in his Word when I was reading the Bible hours later. Either way, be sure that God heard you!

The point of the exercise is this: The more you talk with God, the more you'll be able to recognize how he speaks to your heart, and the more you'll discover that he offers a place where you can freely and safely express your emotions to him.

See God as Your Heavenly Father

When you get ready to spend time with God in prayer, I want you to imagine him as a Father who is excited to see you, with his arms wide open, welcoming you and smiling at you. Imagine that he is looking at you with love and compassion. Even when you have greatly messed up, don't let the false image of an angry father steer you away from God. Instead, run into your loving heavenly Father's arms and say, "Father, I messed up. Please forgive me. Help me make it right."

God will always be the most emotionally safe person for you, because God himself knit you together in your mother's womb (see Psalm 139:13). He knows everything about you. He knows your ins and outs. He knows what makes you feel better. He knows how to talk to you. He knows what you need to hear. What God wants most is for you to come to him, believing that he knows everything about you—the good, the bad, and the ugly. With a heart of love and eyes filled with compassion, your heavenly Father says, *Come, talk to me. Let's work on it together.*

As you take this step in faith, I pray that you feel God's loving, peaceful presence with you through the Holy Spirit. I pray that his presence will cast away any fear. And I pray that as you talk with him and sense his response, you will come to know just how much he cherishes you so that you develop a healthy and strong attachment to him.

2. Transparency

I was once in a meeting with a CEO of a well-known company when I heard his door open and a voice say, "Daddy!" Before I could turn my head, a little boy ran across the office and into the CEO's arms. The CEO continued our meeting with his son right there on his lap. This CEO was highly respected among his staff, and none of them would ever dare to interrupt him as this child did. Why? Because their relationship with him was strictly professional. The CEO's relationship with his child, however, was personal and transparent, which means "free from pretense or deceit."[1]

Personal vs. Professional

As I sat there watching the CEO, it dawned on me: His interactions with his child and staff illustrated the difference between a "personal" relationship with God and a "professional" relationship with God. As

Pastor Timothy Keller once said, "The only person who dares wake up a king at 3:00 a.m. for a glass of water is a child. We have that kind of access."[2]

You see, the reason you're able to run boldly to God is because you are his child—chosen, forgiven, and treasured by him because of Christ's sacrifice on your behalf. So if you have an idea that God is shaking his head at you or raising his fist in anger, I want you to erase that from your mind, because it is completely contrary to who God is. The Word of God says, "God is love" (1 John 4:8)—not "God has love." God *is* the actual definition of love, which means that God is the author of love and the full expression of love.

The reason you're able to run boldly to God is because you are his child–chosen, forgiven, and treasured by him.

The relational dynamics between the CEO, his child, and the staff carry different levels of transparency. The employee understands that his relationship with the CEO is professional. Their meetings take place in a structured setting, where the employee puts his best foot forward because he's trying to please his boss since there is always the possibility he could get fired. And while the child knows that he may get reprimanded, he understands his position is secure in his father's life. He has no qualms about transparently sharing with his father whatever is in his heart or on his mind.

The same concept applies to our relationship with God. Although God is the CEO of the universe, so often we relate to him as employees instead of as his children. Rather than being real with him about what's going on in our lives, we tell God what we think he wants to hear. In other words, we keep our prayer life ... professional. To give you a better understanding of the difference between a professional and a personal relationship with God, take a look at the following chart:

"Professional" Relationship with God	"Personal" Relationship with God
When praying, you're selective with your words and use socially acceptable manners. For example, you close your eyes or pray in a certain posture (like kneeling) because you believe doing so will gain you more favor with God.	You respect God deeply, but you also have confidence in his love for you. You talk freely with him anywhere and anytime about what's going on in your life, no matter how good or bad, and you thank him for all he does for you.
You put your best foot forward and do good works in hopes that God will like you better or love you more.	You understand that because of what Jesus did for you, God accepts you. You know that although he won't leave you the way he found you, you have no ability to change without his help. So you go to him as you are.
You try to hide your flaws and enhance your strengths in an attempt to advance or at least keep yourself from losing favor with God.	Though it may make you uncomfortable, you understand that God wants to help you overcome all that is not good for you. So rather than hiding, you continuously ask him to examine your heart and trust him to lovingly do so.

"God, I'm Hurting"

Often the experiences we go through in life leave us with a sense of shame and prevent us from being transparent with God. For years, I related to God as if he were my employer more so than my Father, and because of that, I shied away from being transparent with him. Honestly, that only made my heart heavier. For years I believed that if I told God how I was truly feeling, he would be angry and allow something bad to happen to me—perhaps even "fire" me from being his child.

Then one day, I could no longer hold in all my pent-up emotions. I mustered my courage and decided to be transparent with God, hoping and praying he wouldn't be disappointed with my emotions—or worse, see me as an ungrateful child. In my anguish, I uttered, "God, I'm hurting." As I proceeded to pour out my heart to him, I remember using the words "I'm scared" and "I need you."

God didn't answer right away, but what I felt was peace. I had gone to God, the CEO of the universe, as my Father. I had told him exactly how I felt, and I trusted him with the outcome. Two days later, I was minding my own business when all of a sudden, memories started flooding my mind of times when

God had delayed certain things or closed certain doors in my life; times when God had brought me through incredibly difficult experiences.

As the memories flooded, I felt a nudge in my stomach—the Holy Spirit reminding me that God the Father knows what he is doing. My responsibility was to just trust him. I was honestly relieved to know that God wasn't mad at me for sharing all my feelings with him, and I was also in awe that he answered in a way that made sense to me personally. My friend, that is how personal God is when we are transparent with him! If you haven't already, I encourage you to complete Exercise 2 ("Believe You Are Forgiven") in the appendix. It offers a wonderful opportunity to be transparent with your heavenly Father.

3. Trust

Just as any child occasionally disobeys his parents, there will likely be times when you act in a way that is inconsistent with the truths and commands in the

Bible. When that happens, you may feel a nudge from the Holy Spirit that seems to communicate, "Hey, you shouldn't have done that—that's not who you are as my child," followed by a nudge to correct your behavior. At this point, your obedience and your trust are on trial, and you have to decide: *Will I keep doing what I know is wrong, even if it feels good? Or will I act in a way that is consistent with the truth about God and myself, then trust him for a better result?*

God's Good Motivation

Over the years, I've heard people share their hesitancy to trust God with the inner core of their heart because they feared that he would "force" them into something they didn't want to do. But rest assured that God is not a dictator. The basis of him wanting you to trust him is for your benefit. As we've discussed, God knows how he made you, and he also knows the good purpose for which he made you. As you grow in your relationship with him and learn to trust him, he will little by little unveil his plan for your life.

A lot of times we think that trusting God means taking huge leaps of faith, like moving far away to serve him in a role we believe he's calling us to. But in reality, trusting God starts with little things, like when you sense he wants you to apologize to someone you spoke rudely to, or to do the right thing when you know you could easily get away with doing the wrong thing.

God knows that having a relationship with him doesn't mean you'll never sin again. But in his loving nature, God will give you course corrections, or "convictions," as a way of bringing you back to who he created you to be. Take comfort in knowing that God's conviction is not the same as condemnation:

- Conviction is motivated by love, for the purpose of correction.
- Condemnation is from Satan, the enemy of our souls, and is motivated by pride, for the purpose of bringing someone down.

God has already justified and forgiven you through Christ, and he is committed to seeing you through. Philippians 1:6 says, "God, who began the good work within you, will continue his work until it is finally finished on the day when Christ Jesus returns" (NLT). Part of his commitment is not only to comfort us when we're hurting but also to correct us when we're wrong and to guide us forward with his wisdom.

We need to be open to receiving God's correction with the understanding that it comes from a place of love that is protective and shows how much we are valued. Only then can we truly be receptive to his love and guidance. Trusting God in this way is a long-term process that may not always make sense. But along the way, we're able to say yes to God with confidence that:

- He cares about our well-being.
- He knows everything about us and yet is committed for the long haul.
- He has our best interest at heart.

■ ■ ■

While writing this book, I came across a Bible verse that summarizes the three layers of secure attachment to God that we just covered. God's timing is incredible, isn't it? The passage is Psalm 62:8:

> *O my people, trust in him [be securely attached to him in full trust] at all times.*
> *Pour out your heart to him [be transparent with him],*
> *for God is our refuge [he is our place of emotional safety].* (NLT)

Are you ready to trust God with your heart? He is fully trustworthy, and he waits ever so patiently and lovingly as you choose to draw near to him.

Your Turn

1. Which prayer-conversation starter did you try, and what were the results?

2. Knowing that God wants to nurture your emotional safety, name an issue you're inspired to be transparent about with him.

3. Describe an area or situation where God may be nudging you to make a correction. What are some reasons to trust him for a good result?

Maintaining a Secure Attachment

Now that we've looked at the process of forming a secure attachment to God one layer at a time, let's talk about some steps that will help you *maintain* a healthy attachment. In life you will go through seasons when you feel close to God and others when you feel far from him, as though your prayers were bouncing off the ceiling. The three steps that follow will help grow your trust in God, regardless of which season you find yourself in.

1. Spend Time with God

Spending time with God is key to maintaining a secure attachment to him. And while activities like going to church and listening to sermons may confirm what you already know about God, they still cannot substitute for one-on-one time. This means getting to know him by talking to him about your needs, fears, hopes, dreams, and desires. It means reading the Bible to learn about his character. Spending time with God can also include journaling your thoughts and feelings after reading a Bible passage, listening to worship music and thanking God for who he is and what he has done for you, or listening to an audio Bible while relaxing.

Correcting Misperceptions

As you interact with God in this way, the comforting presence of the Holy Spirit will grow your assurance of his fatherly love for you, debunking myths you may have picked up about God throughout your childhood. You may be surprised at how many false beliefs you may hold about God—until you spend time with him in his Word and seek him throughout your day.

For me, this process has taken years, and I'm still uncovering false perceptions. Growing up, I believed God was distant, harsh, and unapproachable, but as I read in the Bible how God interacted with people, I noticed a pattern of his unchanging love and faithfulness. His Word spoke to my heart and gently exposed just how mistaken my view of him was.

As I better understood God's true character, spending time with him became something to look forward to rather than a task to be completed. In Jesus I found the love and security that was missing in my childhood—and the same can be true for you.

No Worries about When

The amount of time you spend with God and the time of day you meet with him will likely vary depending on your season of life. For example, when my children were babies and their sleeping habits were all over the place, I didn't have a set schedule for meeting with God. I was tempted to feel ashamed that I wasn't spending as much time with God as I had before, but I quickly remembered that God was not counting every minute and writing it down in some heavenly record book. Rather, he was simply delighted that I was spending time with him. He revealed his character and his thoughts to me during those times, and he showed me his love. As a result, I felt secure in who I was as his child.

> As you spend time with God, the comforting presence of the Holy Spirit will grow your assurance of his fatherly love for you.

2. Include God in Your Decisions

Years ago, my husband, David, and I sensed God calling us to start our own counseling practice. Over the years, many people have asked us to share the secret to our success. Our answer has always been, "We learned early on to include God in our day-to-day decisions." Because we believed God had created us for his own good purposes, we committed our plans to him. We got into the habit of seeking his wisdom in both our personal matters (such as which daycare was right for our children) and our professional decisions (such as whether to hire a particular person).

No decisions are too small for God to be involved. He *wants* to be a part of your daily life. He doesn't want you to come to him only when you're in a crisis. In fact, when you get into the habit of including God in your daily decisions, you're more likely to feel comfortable crying out to him when you're in dire need.

He Gives Wisdom

As children of God, we can avoid many heartaches if we consult him before jumping into something. After all, God is the author of wisdom, and he does not withhold it from his children when they ask. In fact, he promises to give wisdom generously:

- "If any of you lacks wisdom, you should ask God, who gives generously to all without finding fault, and it will be given to you." (James 1:5)
- "The LORD grants wisdom! From his mouth come knowledge and understanding. He grants a treasure of common sense to the honest. He is a shield to those who walk with integrity. He guards the paths of the just and protects those who are faithful to him. Then you will

understand what is right, just, and fair, and you will find the right way to go. For wisdom will enter your heart, and knowledge will fill you with joy. Wise choices will watch over you. Understanding will keep you safe."
(Proverbs 2:6–11 NLT)

He Directs Your Path

As a first step, ask God to guide you in things that may seem menial in terms of spiritual significance. Here is one example: "Father, should I buy these concert tickets, or is there something else you would rather I do instead?" Once you get used to including God in small matters like this one, ask him to help you surrender other areas of your life to his guidance—for example, parenting, marriage, or career.

Sometimes it's necessary to take your feelings out of the equation to gain more wisdom about which way to go. For example, let's say your child insists on exceeding the limits you've placed on screen time or bedtime. It may seem desirable to bend the rules in order to maintain harmony, but taking your emotions out of the equation will help you focus on the more important goal of ensuring consistency and structure in setting boundaries.

If my husband and I don't have clarity about a decision and both directions seem in line with the Bible, we simply choose the option we both feel at peace about, because God is the "Prince of Peace" (Isaiah 9:6). Be assured that if later you regret your decision, then somehow, some way, God's grace is still there to cover you. As Romans 8:28 says, "God causes everything to work together for the good of those who love God and are called according to his purpose" (NLT).

He Is Trustworthy

Because I grew up in a home that frowned upon autonomy, I was reluctant to include God in my day-to-day decisions since I thought he would want to control me. But as I drew closer to God, I realized that wasn't the case. My faith and confidence grew in the reality of God's good motivation—that he truly loves me and has my best interest at heart. I understood that because he is loving, he wanted to be part of my daily decisions—not to control me, but to guide and protect me from my own self-destructive nature.

I believe you also will come to realize this truth as you progress through each layer of attachment. Trusting

God means believing and accepting that his plans are better, even when things don't go our way. Hindsight often reveals the wisdom of his choices, but sometimes we'll never know why he chose a certain path for us. When you find yourself doubting his goodness, it can be beneficial to remind yourself that God's decision to choose you, forgive you, and treasure you was motivated purely by love, not obligation.

At times you will also encounter instances when you *know* God is calling you to do something, but you find bumps along the road. You may be tempted to question, *Did God ask me to do this? If this is truly from God, why is it so hard?* During these times, I encourage you to remember what Jesus said to his disciples in John 16:33: "Here on earth you will have many trials and sorrows. But take heart, because I have overcome the world" (NLT). In other words, through the difficulty God is saying, *I am here with you.* Through the trials he is echoing, *I still have you.* Trusting God's process is surrendering to the fact that we only see in part, while he sees the whole picture.

God's decision to choose you, forgive you, and treasure you was motivated purely by love, not obligation.

I once had a client who was career-driven. She was offered the job of her dreams, but she hesitated because she and her family would need to move to a different state. My client shrugged off the feeling and determined that of course she would move—this was the job of her dreams, after all! Yet her hesitation would not go away, and finally she conceded it wasn't God's will for her to take that opportunity. She trusted God through this process and turned down the offer. Later, the position my client turned down was eliminated. Had she taken it, she would have been left without a job.

> Trusting God's process is surrendering to the fact that we only see in part, while he sees the whole picture.

You see, God knows the future. He sees the beginning and the end. Sometimes God will prompt you to say yes or no to certain things. It's so important to trust him then, knowing he not only has your back but is also guiding you step-by-step through the plan he has set out for you.

HOW CAN I DISCERN GOD'S LEADING?

Sometimes it can be difficult to know what specific path in life God wants you to follow. Here are some hints to help you determine if he is leading you in a certain direction.

- **You feel pulled in a particular direction.** This may include something you're naturally inclined to do, or it could also be something you're not comfortable with and would absolutely need God to help you with. When God called me to the field of counseling, I felt so ill-equipped that I sought prayer from others to make sure the leading was truly from God. The pull became stronger until I made the decision to pursue a counseling degree.

- **You have peace about your decision.** Often this type of peace makes no sense in light of your circumstances. For example, in my case, I *hated* the idea of having to go back to school and accumulate student loans. Yet for some reason, I felt at peace about it, although I would never have been okay with it before.
- **You don't have peace about your decision.** In contrast to the previous point, it's possible to feel uneasy about a decision that would usually seem like a no-brainer to you. In this circumstance, it's so important to remember that God sees the whole picture, while you see only in part. There is a reason you feel uneasy, and God may choose to reveal it to you now, later, or not at all. But what you can count on is that God will never lead you wrong. It's better to back off from your plans rather than risk going in the wrong direction.
- **You notice a shift in your circumstances.** God will open doors (even ones that may seem impossible to open) to bring about his will in your life. And when you don't want to budge, he will often close doors in your present circumstances to get you where he wants you. When the Lord nudged my

husband and I to open our own counseling practice, I was working for someone else's practice. I was comfortable there, and it was debilitating to think about leaving my comfort zone to start from scratch. Then the Lord allowed a period of time when I experienced negative circumstances where I was working. It was not fun, but looking back, I understand that God was allowing me to get uncomfortable so I would move on to where he wanted me. Now, years later, God has grown our practice and granted us success. The road hasn't been easy, but my husband and I have learned to lean on God more and more. I have even paid off the student loans I accumulated. Where God guides, God provides. You can count on his love and faithfulness to carry you through.

3. Build Healthy Friendships

In addition to spending time with God and including him in your decisions, it's important to surround yourself with Christian friends who can help strengthen your attachment to God. Often we shy away from healthy friendships because we've experienced so much betrayal, leaving us with an attitude of "I only need Jesus." But when life knocks you down, having friends who will pray for you and inspire you with their faith is crucial.

A powerful account of this kind of friendship is found in Mark 2:1–12 and Luke 5:17–26. A certain man was paralyzed, so his friends carried him on a mat and took him to Jesus. A big crowd had gathered, blocking the way to Jesus, so they dug a hole in the roof of the house where Jesus was ministering. They lowered the man right down to Jesus, and Jesus was so amazed by the faith of these friends that he forgave the man's sins and healed him.

Choosing Wisely

When we are weak, we, too, need friends who will, so to speak, cut a hole through the roof to bring us to Jesus. But it's important to choose our friends wisely. When people eagerly receive what we offer them through friendship but don't make an effort to reciprocate what we have invested, we end up feeling used. It's also easy to fall into bad friendships because we want someone to meet a need that really only God can fill. That's yet another reason why it's so important that our relationship with God be foundational above all others. He alone speaks to our identity, which fosters the confidence and security we need to build healthy relationships with others. As you seek to identify which people God has strategically placed in your life for mutual encouragement, consider *character, variety,* and *confirmation.*

Character

Proverbs 12:26 says, "The righteous choose their friends carefully, but the way of the wicked leads them astray." A friend has the potential to either help or hinder your ability to have a healthy attachment with God. In choosing an inner circle of friends, it's helpful to assess a person's character by asking yourself the following questions:

- *Do I feel closer to God after I hang out with this person?*
- *Does this person encourage me toward a closer walk with God?*

- *Would this person love me enough to hold me accountable when I mess up, then show me grace and pray for me as I take corrective measures?*
- *When this person is the one in the wrong, does he or she take steps to make things right?*

No friend is perfect. The point is to help you discern whether the person you're inviting into your life is good for you or bad for you. If this person constantly makes you feel drained or condemned for making a mistake, or if he or she encourages you to live in a way that is contrary to God's desires for you, ask God to help you find a better friend. Jesus died to give you freedom and joy, so it follows that he wants you to have life-giving friends who point you toward him.

> It's easy to fall into bad friendships because we want someone to meet a need that only God can fill.

Variety

Throughout your life, it's ideal to maintain a variety of friendships since one person is not equipped to meet every need. Just as you would go to a cardiologist and not an eye doctor if you're having problems with your heart, it's important that you seek care from the right person when it comes to your spiritual heart. For example, if you're a mom seeking advice as your kids are about to start school, first ask for guidance from the Holy Spirit, who knows the will of God, and then consult a friend who loves God and is years ahead or in a similar season of raising children. Or if you are part of a Bible study group with friends who are in different seasons of life, it won't make sense to ask for help with areas you've never shared in common, but you can certainly ask for prayer support.

Confirmation

As you seek the support of Christian friends, some who are well-meaning may approach you and say, "God told me to tell you this" or "God said you should do this." It's important to be aware that just because someone is a Christian does not necessarily mean they're speaking for God. They may or may not be, and it's also possible their message contains nuggets of truth but doesn't fully capture what God wants to communicate to you. This is why, as you seek to make decisions, it's so important that your primary source of wisdom be God himself as you spend time with him in prayer and Bible reading. If you have committed your life to Jesus, God has put the Holy Spirit in you to lead you, so he doesn't need to go through a friend to send you a message. However,

God may choose to use a friend to *confirm* what he has already put in your heart. As you learn to follow his leading, keep in mind that it will never contradict his Word, the Bible.

■ ■ ■

The topic of a secure attachment with God is meaningful for you personally and important for your mental health. I hope you've enjoyed reading *Secure* as much as I have enjoyed writing it. As you continue your journey to develop a secure attachment to God, know that I have prayed for you these words:

> I ask God to give you complete knowledge of his will and to give you spiritual wisdom and understanding. Then the way you live will always honor and please the Lord, and your life will produce every kind of good fruit. All the while, you will grow as you learn to know God better and better. I also pray that you will be strengthened with all his glorious power, so you will have all the endurance and patience you need. May you be filled with joy, always thanking the Father. He has enabled you to share in the inheritance that belongs to his people, who live in the light. *Amen!* (adapted from Colossians 1:9–12 NLT)

Your Turn

1. What are some hopes, dreams, problems, fears, or desires you're looking forward to sharing with God when you spend time with him?

2. What upcoming decisions can you ask God to help you with? Here is an example of how you can pray: *Father, you are the author of wisdom. I confess there are times when I rush to make a decision on my own without including you. Moving forward, Father, I want to include you in every area of my life. Please show me your will as I seek your guidance about ____________. Order my steps according to your will, and help me to follow your lead. In Jesus's name, amen.*

3. Think of a time when you formed a friendship that wasn't good for you. What factors contributed to making it unhealthy? Write a prayer asking God to send a variety of friends who will support you in specific areas of your life.

Appendix
Exercises to Grow Your Attachment to God

EXERCISE 1
Know God as a Loving Father

As mentioned in chapter 2, I walked Jon through an exercise to help him process unresolved trauma from his childhood and develop a secure attachment to God. Following are instructions for working through this exercise on your own, either directly on the page or in your own journal.

1. **Unhealthy Parent Characteristic:** For each unhealthy parent characteristic, write down

any ways you may have experienced this behavior as you were growing up.

2. **Truth about God the Father:** Rewrite the corresponding truth about God, or expand on it in your own words.

3. **Bible Passage:** Read the Bible passage out loud or quietly to yourself. I've found the best way to let God's Word sink into my heart is by substituting my name where needed to make it personally applicable. You may want to do the same.

Emotionally Unavailable

1. How I Experienced This Parent Characteristic

2. Truth about God the Father

He gives me his undivided attention.

3. Bible Passage

Psalm 139:1–3: "*You have searched me,* Lord, *and you know me. You know when I sit and when I rise;*

you perceive my thoughts from afar. You discern my going out and my lying down; you are familiar with all my ways."

Emotionally Dismissive

1. How I Experienced This Parent Characteristic

2. Truth about God the Father

He welcomes me with all my emotions.

3. Bible Passages

1 Peter 5:7: "*Cast all your anxiety on him because he cares for you.*"

Psalm 34:18: "*The Lord is close to the brokenhearted and saves those who are crushed in spirit.*"

Overemphasis on Independence

1. How I Experienced This Parent Characteristic

2. Truth about God the Father

He is the author of wisdom. He invites me to come to him for wisdom and guidance.

3. Bible Passages

James 1:5: "*If any of you lacks wisdom, you should ask God, who gives generously to all without finding fault, and it will be given to you.*"

Psalm 32:8: "*I will instruct you and teach you in the way you should go; I will counsel you with my loving eye on you.*"

Clinginess

1. How I Experienced This Parent Characteristic

2. Truth about God the Father

God's pursuit is lovingly meant to free me from self-condemnation.

3. Bible Passage

John 8:36: *"If the Son sets you free, you will be free indeed."*

Overemphasis on Performance

1. How I Experienced This Parent Characteristic

2. Truth about God the Father

God is the one who accomplishes good things in me.

3. Bible Passage

John 15:5: *"I am the vine; you are the branches. If you remain in me and I in you, you will bear much fruit; apart from me you can do nothing."*

High Anxiety

1. How I Experienced This Parent Characteristic

2. Truth about God the Father

God wants me to share in his peace.

3. Bible Passage

Philippians 4:6–7: "*In every situation, by prayer and petition, with thanksgiving, present your requests to God. And the peace of God, which transcends all understanding, will guard your hearts and your minds in Christ Jesus.*"

Unpredictable Mood Swings

1. How I Experienced This Parent Characteristic

2. Truth about God the Father

God is safe, unchanging, and faithful. He will never suddenly turn against me.

3. Bible Passage

Hebrews 6:18 NLT: "*God has given both his promise and his oath. These two things are unchangeable because it is impossible for God to lie. Therefore, we who have fled to him for refuge can have great confidence as we hold to the hope that lies before us.*"

Role Reversal

1. How I Experienced This Parent Characteristic

2. Truth about God the Father

God wants to carry my burdens. He offers me a safe space to share them with him.

3. Bible Passage

Matthew 11:28–30: "*Come to me, all you who are weary and burdened, and I will give you rest. Take my yoke upon you and learn from me, for I am gentle and humble in heart, and you will find rest for your souls. For my yoke is easy and my burden is light.*"

Frequent Criticism and Praise

1. How I Experienced This Parent Characteristic

2. Truth about God the Father

God's love for me does not depend on my good behavior.

3. Bible Passages

Romans 5:8: "*While we were still sinners, Christ died for us.*"

Romans 8:38–39: "*I am convinced that neither death nor life, neither angels nor demons, neither the present nor the future, nor any powers, neither height nor depth, nor anything else in all creation, will be able to separate us from the love of God that is in Christ Jesus our Lord.*"

EXERCISE 2
Believe You Are Forgiven

Like Ashley from chapter 2, it's possible that when you try to get past your past, people in your present may remind you of past mistakes. The following exercise helps you take those mistakes straight to God, the merciful judge who, because of what Jesus did, has already forgiven you.

---

1. Write down past mistakes that continue to haunt you regardless of how much you've repented (turned away from them).

2. For each one, pray: "Thank you, heavenly Father, for forgiving me for ______________________. I ask that you would remind me of the truth about who I am in you, because of what Jesus did to pay the penalty for my sins and mistakes. When others treat me in a way that makes me feel inferior, please open my eyes to see myself the way you see me—pure, clean, and justified—just as if I had never sinned. In Jesus's name, amen."

3. Read and meditate on the following personalized Bible passages. They will help you see yourself as you truly are: completely forgiven by God. It's beneficial to repeat these passages so they become part of your inner monologue.

- "God made me alive with Christ, for he forgave all my sins. He canceled the record of the charges against me and took it away by nailing it to the cross." (Colossians 2:13–14 NLT, adapted)
- "I am no longer condemned before God because I belong to Jesus." (Romans 8:1 NLT, adapted)
- "God has removed my sins as far from me as the east is from the west." (Psalm 103:12 NLT, adapted)

Acknowledgments

To my editor, Anisa Larramore, and my marketing manager at Tyndale House, Steph Bradac: Your enthusiasm and dedication have been a true gift. To my husband, David, and my children, Benjamin and Eliza: Thank you for your constant support and encouragement. Thank you, Jesus.

About the Author

Kenza Haddock, LPCS, BCPC, is a licensed professional counselor supervisor and an accredited clinical trauma specialist with expertise in treating complex mental health conditions through both clinical and biblical methods. A former Muslim, she has spoken at conferences and churches and has been featured in numerous media outlets regarding the intersection of Christianity and mental health counseling. Haddock and her husband own Oceanic Counseling Group LLC, an outpatient mental health agency headquartered in South Carolina.

Notes

1 *Merriam-Webster Dictionary*, "transparent," *https://www.merriam-webster.com/dictionary/transparent.*

2 Timothy Keller, Facebook, December 3, 2019, *https://www.facebook.com/TimKellerNYC/posts/the-only-person-who-dares-wake-up-a-king-at-300-am-for-a-glass-of-water-is-a-chi/2799625540077314/.*

Hope and Healing

Unmasking Emotional Abuse

Six Steps to Reduce Stress

Ten Tips for Parenting the Smartphone Generation

Five Keys to Dealing with Depression

Seven Answers for Anxiety

Five Keys to Raising Boys

Freedom From Shame

Five Keys to Health and Healing

When a Loved One Is Addicted

Social Media and Depression

Rebuilding Trust after Betrayal

How to Deal with Toxic People

The Power of Connection

Why Failure Is Never Final

Find Your Purpose in Life

Here Today, Ghosted Tomorrow

Caregiving

Forgiveness

Mental Illness

Secure